This book belongs to:

____

A
Autism

B
Behavior

C
Communication

D
Disorder
(ASD)

E
Echo
(Echolalia)

F

Genetics

H
Hugs?

I
IEP
Individual Educational
Program

J
Joy

K
Kind

L
Laugh

M
Maintain Routine

N
Neurological

O
Our Family

P
Patience

Q
Questions
(Ask them)

R
Repeat

S
Social Interaction

T
Therapy

U
Understanding

Visual Learning

W
Walk

eXtra Love

Y
No Yelling

Z
amazing
You're
AMAZING